101 HO-HO-HOLIDAY JOKES

by H. N. Kowitt
Illustrated by Donna Reynolds

Scholastic Inc.

ISBN 978-0-545-46134-4

Copyright © 2012 by Scholastic Inc.

All rights reserved. Published by Scholastic Inc.

SCHOLASTIC and associated logos are
trademarks and/or registered trademarks
of Scholastic Inc.

18 17   17 18 19/0

Printed in the U.S.A.   23

First Scholastic printing, November 2012

Why is Santa good at karate?

He has a black belt.

When does Serena Williams use a turkey instead of a tennis ball?

When she's serving Christmas dinner.

What do cannibals do on New Year's Day?

They have friends for lunch.

Why didn't the snowman perform in the Christmas pageant?

He got cold feet.

How do you know if Santa Claus is in the house?

You can sense his presents.

Where do werewolves buy Christmas gifts?

Beast Buy.

How did the rhinoceros celebrate New Year's?

By blowing his horn.

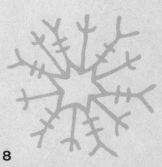

How can you tell that elves admire Santa?

They look up to him.

Knock, knock.
Who's there?
Yule.
Yule who?

Yule be sorry if you eat all the fruitcake!

Knock, knock.
Who's there?
Cheddar.
Cheddar who?

"You cheddar watch out, you cheddar not cry. . ."

What did the snowflake say to the road?

"Let's stick together."

Why did the boy stop practicing the violin at Christmas?

Because his mother asked for peace on Earth.

How does Santa call his toys to bed?

"Time to hit the sack!"

Did the blizzard damage your house?

No, everything turned out all white.

Icicle #1: Why'd you break up with your boyfriend?

Icicle #2: He was a real drip.

Why do you learn something at Christmas dinner?

Because there are several courses.

What do elves read?

Short stories.

Why didn't the pig go to the Christmas party?

It wasn't in the mud.

What does Sir Lancelot recite on December 24?

"'Twas the Knight Before Christmas."

Did you hear about the Christmas shopper who'd buy anything marked down?

She came home with an elevator.

Knock, knock.
Who's there?
Good-byes.
Good-byes who?

Good buys at the mall before Christmas.

What does Santa do at football games?

He gives a little Christmas cheer.

What's Frosty the Snowman's favorite song?

"There's No Business Like Snow Business."

Why did the reindeer go to the orthodontist?

He had buck teeth.

Why did the turkey join a band?

So he could use his drumsticks.

Why did the karate teacher go to the mall?

To do his Christmas chopping.

Knock, knock.
Who's there?
Latke.
Latke who?

Latke laughs, telling Hanukkah jokes.

Where did Santa study?

At a school for the gifted.

Why couldn't the skunk pay for the gift he bought?

He only had one scent, and it was bad.

What did Homer Simpson say when he dressed like Santa?

"D'oh, d'oh, d'oh!"

Monster #1: Am I late for Christmas dinner?

Monster #2: Yes, everyone's eaten.

What's a math teacher's favorite winter sport?

Figure skating.

What does Godzilla do on New Year's Eve?

He steps out on the town.

What do you get when you sprinkle salt on Christmas cards?

Seasoned greetings.

Why did the dumb guy throw away the guitar he got for Christmas?

It had a hole in the middle.

What does a clock do after Christmas dinner?

It goes back four seconds.

Why did the Blob eat a string of Christmas bulbs?

He wanted a light snack.

Mary: My Christmas candy is missing.

Terry: That's too bad, because it tasted delicious.

Where do snowmen keep their money?

In a snowbank.

What do aliens like in their hot chocolate?

Martian-mallows.

Why did the dumb guy bring a hammer on Christmas vacation?

He wanted to hit the road.

How do you spell "cold" with two letters?

"I-C."

Why do pigs go to the mall in December?

They do their Christmas slopping.

Dumb: Why'd you bring a shovel to Christmas dinner?

Dumber: You said to dig in!

What's the best thing to put in a pumpkin pie?

Your teeth!

Why did Jenna wear pine boughs to the fancy party?

She heard all the women would be wearing fir.

What cereal do snowmen eat?

Frosted flakes.

Why did Rudolph go to the library?

He's well-red.

What do teachers drink on snowy days?

Hot chalk-olate.

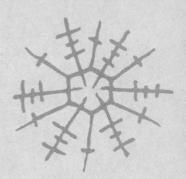

What are Santa's favorite snacks?

Ho Hos.

Knock, knock.
Who's there?
Snow.
Snow who?

'S no way I'm going out in this weather!

What happened to the angry snowman?

He had a meltdown.

Why didn't the elephant fly home for Christmas?

Last time, the airline lost his trunk.

Why did the elf join a baseball team?

They needed a shortstop.

Knock, knock.
Who's there?
Icy.
Icy who?

Icy your underwear!

How does Scrooge begin every story?

"Once upon a dime . . ."

What does Santa use to help him walk?

A candy cane.

Where do leopards buy their Christmas gifts?

From cat-alogs.

Knock, knock
Who's there?
Freeze.
Freeze who?

"Freeze a jolly good fellow . . ."

What do hip-hop singers like about Christmas?

Rapping presents.

What do you call a piece of snow that forgets to fall?

A flake.

What do they serve at the North Pole McDonald's?

Brrrr-gers.

Where do ghosts do their holiday shopping?

Chain stores.

What did one Hanukkah candle say to another?

"Want to go out tonight?"

Why did the golfer buy two Christmas stockings?

In case he got a hole in one.

Why did the dumb guy go to the bank on December 26?

He got cash as a gift and wanted to exchange it.

What did the film director say when she saw the gift ribbon?

"Cut!"

Who is the cleanest reindeer?

Comet.

How do vampires sign their holiday cards?

"Best vicious."

Teacher: Why are you tearing December off the calendar?

Boy: I wanted to take the month off.

What happened to the boy who swallowed Christmas decorations?

He got tinsel-litis.

What do you call an old snowman?

Water.

What do you get when pelicans go Christmas shopping?

A big bill.

What do you serve a frog on Christmas?

A cup of hot spider.

Why couldn't the snowball take a trip?

It wasn't packed yet.

Mrs. Claus: How much did you pay for that sleigh?

Santa: Nothing. It was on the house!

How did the Christmas tree feel after the beaver left?

Gnawed so good.

Why don't kids at the North Pole go to school?

Because every day's a snow day!

What's a snowman's favorite meal?

Chili.

Why couldn't the elf pay for his groceries?

He was a little short.

Why did the bird sing after Christmas dinner?

He wanted more tweets.

What does a snowman sleep on?

Sheets of ice.

Knock, knock.
Who's there?
Santa.
Santa who?

Santa gift in the mail—hope you got it!

Why didn't the skeleton go to the New Year's dance?

He had no body to go with.

What did the snake do under the mistletoe?

He gave his girlfriend a hiss.

Santa: What's the weather forecast for today?

Mrs. Claus: Looks like rain, dear.

Why didn't the turkey eat his dinner?

He was already stuffed.

Which reindeer is the smartest?

Rudolph. He's very bright.

Where do TVs go for Christmas vacation?

To remote places.

What did the bald man say when he got a comb for Christmas?

"I'll never part with it!"

Girl: I'd like an iPod for my brother.

Clerk: Sorry, we don't do trades.

What do grapes sing at Christmas?

" 'Tis the season to be jelly . . ."

Ben: There's something wrong with that dessert I ate.

Jen: How do you know?

Ben: Inside information.

Why did the girl tell jokes at the skating party?

To break the ice.

What does Santa do in the spring?

Hoe, hoe, hoe.

Why did Santa's sleigh turn left?

Because the sign said "Bear Right."

Where does Dracula shop for Christmas gifts?

Bed Bat & Beyond.

What do witches serve on Christmas?

A three-curse meal.

Kid: For Christmas, I'd like some things that are hard to break.

Mother: Plastic toys?

Kid: No, hundred-dollar bills.

What do snowmen like about cake?

The icing.

Knock, knock.
Who's there?
Irish.
Irish who?

"Irish you a Merry Christmas!"